Original title:
Lemon and Lace

Copyright © 2025 Creative Arts Management OÜ
All rights reserved.

Author: Rafael Sterling
ISBN HARDBACK: 978-1-80586-313-7
ISBN PAPERBACK: 978-1-80586-785-2

A Citrus Serenade on Gentle Fabrics

A zesty dance upon the seams,
Where bright and cheerful playfulness beams.
Stitches chuckle, fabric grins,
As colors swirl like joyful twins.

Wrap me in your citrus cheer,
With a touch that's oh so near.
Threads of sunshine spark delight,
In a world where smiles ignite.

Threads of Gold Against a Whispered Breeze

Golden threads are weaving tales,
As breezes laugh and play like gales.
Whispers soft, they spin and twine,
In laughter's glow, our hearts align.

Stitches stitched with playful flair,
Bantering with the sun-soaked air.
A playful hug, a fabric wink,
In this dance, we laugh and blink.

Hues of Joy entwined in a Tangle

Bright hues twirl in comical knots,
As laughter spills from all the spots.
A tapestry of giggles we weave,
Where silly patterns will not leave.

In tangled threads, we find our fun,
A carnival dance beneath the sun.
Every knot, a joke well-told,
In this fabric of humor, bold.

Tantalizing Brightness in Woven Memories

Memories are stitched with radiance,
Bright moments dance in a merry stance.
Each thread whispers of wild delight,
Creating tales that twinkle bright.

Remember when we laughed so loud?
Sewn into time, our joy allowed.
With every stitch, a smile we find,
A quilt of laughter, joy entwined.

Citrus Whispers in Gossamer Threads

In a garden bright with mischief's tease,
   Frolicking scents float in the breeze.
  Fabric spun from giggles and light,
    Sparkling fruits dance in delight.

The sun chuckles, baking with glee,
   Tickling petals on the nearby tree.
Threads of humor, so vivid and bright,
Stitching together the day and the night.

Tangy Radiance on Delicate Fabric

A splash of brightness spills from the cup,
As stitches giggle, won't give up.
A tapestry woven, sweet and tart,
Crafting joy that warms the heart.

Fabric soft, with winks and grins,
Bubbles of laughter, where the fun begins.
Colors dance like playful sprites,
Spreading cheer on cloudless nights.

Golden Zest and Frayed Edges

With frayed edges that tease and play,
In the twilight, they sway away.
Bright zest hidden in folds so fine,
Whispers of giggles in every line.

Unexpected laughs from every seam,
A patchwork of joy, a quirky dream.
In silly patterns, life's little quirks,
Light-hearted laughter as the fabric jerks.

Bright Elixirs in Soft Embrace

In bowls of sunshine, joy is brewed,
With playful sips, laughter accrued.
Fabrics embrace the giggles released,
A whimsical party, never ceased.

Softness wrapped 'round every jest,
Taking life's tang with zest and jest.
Threads of laughter, brightening days,
In this funny dance, joy forever stays.

Enchanted Threads

In a garden where giggles bloom,
Dresses sway to a fragrant tune.
Buttons bounce like playful bees,
Spinning tales with every breeze.

Hats adorned with plump, bright cheer,
Tickled with joy, they draw us near.
Each stitch whispers silly dreams,
As laughter dances, or so it seems.

Melody of Golden Strings

A banter of blooms in the air,
Strings of sunshine everywhere.
Cotton candy clouds float by,
As butterflies join in the sky.

Socks that sing with every hop,
Twirl around, and never stop.
Chasing shadows, bright and bold,
In threads of glee, our joys unfold.

Softly Zesty Stitches

Sprinkles of zest in the breeze,
Crafting smiles with perfect ease.
Pies that giggle, hats that shine,
Oh, what fun is truly divine!

A splash of fun on every seam,
Whispers tickle like a dream.
In this patch of bright delight,
Laughs bloom like stars at night.

Woven Whimsy

A tapestry of joy we weave,
In every hug, we dare believe.
With twinkling eyes and silly grins,
The joy of life begins, it spins.

Breezy skirts that rustle low,
Dancing to the zany flow.
Each knot a chuckle that we share,
A world of whimsy everywhere.

Stitched Sunbeams

A twist of yellow in the air,
With giggles woven everywhere.
Sassy threads of laughter gleam,
Chasing every silly dream.

Jumpsuits bright like morning rays,
Dancing through the sunny maze.
Whimsical stitches that make you grin,
Every flaw a badge to win.

Draped in Radiance

A splash of brightness on a drab day,
As giggly colors come out to play.
Wobbling hats and mismatched socks,
Ticklish toes and silly knocks.

With every beam of light in sight,
Comes frolic with a wink so bright.
The joy unfurls just like a flag,
In quirky tunes and happy brag.

Melodic Citrus Waves

Waves of zest roll in with flair,
Tickling noses in the air.
Dancing curls with lemon drops,
Giggles pop like fizzy tops.

Songs of folly, bright and bold,
Tales of jests yet to be told.
A chorus of chuckles in the sun,
Where silly chaos is pure fun.

Threads of Joy

Tangled yarns of bright delights,
Weaving tales of silly sights.
Each little loop a playful spark,
Creating giggles in the dark.

With every tug a laugh takes flight,
Turning woes into sheer delight.
Life's a quilt of cheerful fray,
Where laughter's stitches never stray.

Whimsical Twists of Fruit and Finesse

In a garden with a twist, where jests abound,
A fruity fairytale made of laughter is found.
Dancing round the citrus, the zest takes the stage,
With giggles and grins, they all turn the page.

The twirling of peels, a sight quite absurd,
Puns roll off the tongue, like yellow-furred birds.
Juicy jokes pop out, one after another,
In this playful circus, we cheer for each other.

Lively Sips Caught in Tidal Layers.

A glass on the table, a splash and a swirl,
Sips full of giggles, let's give it a whirl.
The lemons they sing, with a zesty refrain,
While laughter flows freely, like a sweet sugary rain.

Straws bouncing like whales, in tides of delight,
We stir up the blend, making flavors take flight.
With every small sip, a chuckle takes form,
And inside this delight, we weather the storm.

Sunshine Threads

In threads of bright sunlight, we frolic and weave,
With citrusy humor, oh, how we believe.
Dresses are swirling, twirling with glee,
As laughter and colors dance wildly and free.

Golden rays mingle with gags in the air,
A playful embroidery, vibrant and rare.
Stitching up smiles, through seams they do flow,
In this bright tapestry, we're always in tow.

Citrus Serenade

A serenade hums in the orchard's warm glow,
With tunes full of laughter, we dance to the flow.
Notes twist like corkscrews, bright flavors unfold,
Creating sweet melodies worth more than gold.

Charming and cheery, the verses will cheer,
As the scent of the zingers tickles the ear.
With a rhythm that pops, let us all join in,
In this citrusy symphony, let joy be the win.

Starlit Citrus Night

Under the moon, a fruit parade,
They dance in yellow, bits of shade.
The peels fly high, like kites in glee,
A zestful night, just you and me.

With sparkling drinks in cups that sway,
The fruit confetti hardly stays.
A twist, a giggle, laughter shared,
Who knew a fruit could be so weird?

Stars wink down, as they play charades,
The tangy fruit joins in cascades.
In every drop, a splash of cheer,
Tonight's the night, we've shed our fear.

So raise your glass, let's share the fun,
With citrus friends, we've surely won.
In this bright glow, we'll dance till dawn,
A frolic tale, forever drawn.

Tantalizing Tapestry

A cloth adorned with threads of zest,
Woven stories that make us jest.
Beneath the sun, we stitch and snare,
Fashioning laughter with a citrus flair.

The stitches pop with vibrant hues,
As playful patterns spin the news.
In every corner, a chuckle hides,
With quirky shapes and frothy rides.

We wrap ourselves in sweetness bold,
With tangy tales that never get old.
A fabric light with giggles spun,
Draped in sunshine, just for fun.

So come and join this crafty spree,
With every snip, we're wild and free.
Together we'll weave a joyous fate,
In this sweet tale, let's celebrate.

Honeyed Ribbons

With ribbons tied and bows that sway,
The sticky sweets come out to play.
In golden strands, the laughter flows,
A sugary dance, where nobody knows.

The surprises twist like candy canes,
In every curl, a giggle reigns.
A splash of honey, a dash of fun,
We'll twist our way 'til the day is done.

Each ribbon bright, a silly jest,
The flavor sparkles, never rests.
From tangled loops, we find delight,
In every knot, a joyful sight.

So come and taste this playful glee,
As we unravel, just you and me.
The honeyed sweetness, the laughter shared,
In this whimsical dance, always prepared.

Sun-Kissed Twirls of Fragile Beauty

In gardens bright, a twist of sun,
The blooms get giggly, oh what fun.
With petals swirling, dancing light,
They tickle bees, a sheer delight.

They sip from dew, that sweetened brew,
With laughter spilled, in morning's hue.
A waltz of colors, light as air,
Who knew such joy could bloom so rare?

The breeze joins in, a playful shove,
With every twirl, it's time to love.
Like spinning tops, they whir around,
A charming ballet on soft ground.

So let us dance, in shades so bright,
With fragile beauty, hearts take flight.
And when the day begins to wane,
We'll laugh and frolic once again.

Sweet Citrus Dreams in Silken Veils

A splash of zest, a curtain's swing,
Through fragiles glides a jovial fling.
In silken layers, dreams unite,
A citrus melody, pure delight.

The sunbeams giggle, teasingly shy,
As if they know just how to fly.
Through fragrant lanes, where whispers play,
Come join the dance, don't hide away.

A frothy wave of sparkling cheer,
Horizon twinkles, far and near.
With laughter echoing, sweet and bold,
These silken nights are joys untold.

As starlight dips into the scene,
We savor moments, light and keen.
Wrapped in warmth, let's chase the gleam,
In this bright world, we dare to dream.

A Dance of Sours and Sheens

Twisty worlds where flavors clash,
A wink of tang, a playful splash.
With every bite, a zesty cheer,
In sours and sheens, we disappear.

The jester's hat, a citrus crown,
As giggles burst, and sorrows drown.
Through playful flips, in shadows play,
The sour dance leads hearts astray.

Wobbling fruits, they roll and spin,
Each laugh a note of joy within.
They harmonize, a zany tune,
Under the watchful eye of moon.

With every twirl, our spirits rise,
A party brewed beneath the skies.
In colorful chaos, we combine,
Sours and sheens, our souls align.

Juicy Echoes Amidst Thrumming Stoff

A tumble of colors, beats align,
Juicy echoes dance on a vine.
With laughter bursting, loud and clear,
In this light frenzy, we adhere.

A cocoon of cloth that flutters wide,
Where giggles twist and secrets hide.
Threads of stories on laughter's loom,
With every thread, we weave the bloom.

Waves of sweetness, pure delight,
In thrumming rhythms, night takes flight.
We drink in joy, let worries stray,
This thrilling fabric shouts hooray!

So join the revel, don't stand still,
With every twirl, we chase the thrill.
In juicy rhythms, let's embrace,
The echoes pulse in vibrant space.

Twisted Citrus Dreams

In a garden filled with zest,
Sour faces make a jest.
Twisting like a playful vine,
Citrusy giggles intertwine.

Sunshine spills in orange rays,
Bouncing through the silly ways.
Fruit hats dance upon their heads,
As laughter sprinkles where it spreads.

Wobbling, they play leapfrog,
Through misty paths with a fog.
Whirlwinds of laughter twirl around,
In this fruit-filled, funny ground.

With every twist, a chuckle bursts,
Sourness quenched by laughter's thirst.
Dreams of tang and sweet delight,
Make the world so very bright.

Shimmering Sunbeams

Golden beams break through the trees,
Tickling noses, swaying leaves.
A sparkle in the morning dew,
Chasing shadows, not a clue.

Dancing rays on puddles pop,
Like giggles from a soda shop.
Bright and bouncy, every grin,
In a world where laughs begin.

Jumping jigs upon the grass,
Where the little fireflies pass.
They wear hats of sunny cheer,
Lighting up the day so clear.

Citrus spritz fills the air,
With every laugh, the sun lays bare.
Shimmering through the playful scene,
Everything feels so serene.

Sweet Fragrance of Joy

A scent floats through the lively space,
Bringing smiles to every face.
Sticky fingers from the treat,
Making every moment sweet.

In the air, a playful blend,
Where zany meets and joys transcend.
Curly straws and silly hats,
Spinning tales of friendly chats.

Squirrels giggle, birds all sing,
As the sun begins to swing.
Fruits juggle in a bright parade,
A frolic that will never fade.

Joy spills forth like bubbling cheer,
In the world we hold so dear.
Each sweet whiff a funny rhyme,
Woven through the taste of time.

Whispered Threads

In the fabric of a sunny day,
Whispers tickle, come what may.
Threads of fun, all intertwined,
In silly patterns, joy we find.

Giggling stitches join the seams,
Sewing together all our dreams.
Yarns of laughter fill the air,
With every knot, love is laid bare.

A tapestry of cheerful deeds,
Crafted from our laughter's seeds.
Loop and swirl, a vibrant lace,
Bringing smiles to every face.

Colors splash, like paint on walls,
Echoes of mirth in joyful calls.
In these threads, a world so bold,
With every story yet untold.

Tangy Sunbeams on Whispered Taffeta

Bright rays bounce on fabric soft,
Like zesty dreams that dance aloft.
A giggle wraps the playful day,
As shadows twirl, then skip away.

Sour notes in jokes unfold,
While laughter drips like honey gold.
Threads in chaos, colors clash,
A taffeta job that turns to trash.

Puns like ribbons twist and sway,
In this light, they come to play.
With every chuckle, bright and bold,
Sweetness mixed with tales retold.

So let the sunbeam have its fun,
In woven tales, we're never done.
For life's a patchwork, bright and wise,
Where every glance, a sweet surprise.

The Citrus Caress of Feathery Touch

A poke of zest, a squish, a squeeze,
As laughter floats upon the breeze.
The tickle of a feather's brush,
Turns serious moments into a rush.

Whimsy lies in citrus peels,
With giggles crafting funny reels.
A dance of touch, a playful tease,
Creating joy with perfect ease.

The splash of color on a whim,
Makes every giggle seem like hymn.
With feathery lightness in the air,
We craft our dreams without a care.

So let the citrus tickle your nose,
And fill your heart with silly prose.
In feathery joy, we glide and sway,
Chasing our troubles far away.

Sweetly Etched in Filigree Shadows

Etched in light, a dance unfolds,
The shadows play, a tale retold.
Filigree whispers, soft and sly,
With every giggle, spirits fly.

Sweet delights in patterned grace,
As laughter carves a joyful space.
Winks and nods in designs that tease,
We celebrate, with utmost ease.

Oh, what fun in artful twirls,
As humor wraps like ribbons, swirls.
The filigree shimmers, then it winks,
As shadows plot and laughter links.

In this playground of lovely sights,
We chase our dreams on silly flights.
So come and join this joyful spree,
In filigree shadows, wild and free!

Dappled Sunlight on Delicate Weaves

Dappled light through weavings bright,
Turns every moment into delight.
With witticisms spun so tight,
In playful patterns, feels just right.

Each gentle weave a story told,
With brightening threads, we spark the bold.
In every dapple and playful twist,
Lies joy that's too good to resist.

A tangle here, a loopy round,
In humorous fabric, fun is found.
With sunlight twinkling as we talk,
We weave our laughter, walk the walk.

So join the dance, the playful tease,
In delicate weaves, do what you please.
The sunlight dances, colors gleam,
In dappled joy, we craft a dream.

Garden of Bright Hues

In a patch so lively and spry,
Giggles bloom as colors fly.
Yellow pants on buzzing bees,
Sipping joy from drinkable teas.

Marigolds dancing in a sway,
Tickling cheeks in the sun's play.
A jester's hat on a crooked vine,
Whispering secrets of the divine.

Laughter shimmers, a bright delight,
Even weeds wear a coat of light.
Bumblebees hum a silly tune,
While flowers gossip beneath the moon.

Sunshine winks with a cheeky grin,
As ants march in a quirky spin.
This garden spills joy, just like a prank,
Each petal a laugh, the heart's own bank.

Ribbons of Flavor

A twist of zest in every wrap,
Tangled flavors, a ticklish trap.
Sweet and sour in a playful dance,
Sipping smiles as taste buds prance.

With a sprinkle of silliness on top,
Chasing clouds that go pop, pop, pop!
Squeeze a joke from the citrus bright,
And watch the kitchen take flight!

Whipping cream with a giggle or two,
Stirring laughter in something new.
Jelly beans in a wobbly line,
Whispering tales of a party divine.

Ribbons of flavor, a carnival treat,
Taste buds dancing to a jig so sweet.
In every bite, a chuckle awaits,
This culinary fest that simply elates.

Vibrant Florals

Petals wear hats of emerald green,
Prancing around in a happy scene.
Butterflies twirl with a wink and a spin,
Dancing blooms in a joyful din.

A flower's giggle is heard in the breeze,
Chasing away grumps with effortless ease.
Crickets chatter in a cheeky spree,
Holding court 'neath the old cherry tree.

Colors clash in a playful mess,
Who wore it best? The sunflower, no less!
Each bud a jester, with tricks to unfold,
Blooming bright tales that never get old.

A bouquet of laughs on this fine day,
Whirling petals in a zany hooray!
In this garden of giggles, life's never bland,
Each floral friend, a comical band.

Soft Sunshower Elegance

Raindrops tap a soft, cheeky beat,
While sunbeams shimmy, oh so sweet.
A glittery dance across leafy greens,
In this light, everything gleans.

Puddles form little funhouse mirrors,
Reflecting smiles and silly cheers.
A sprinkle of laughter hangs in the air,
As umbrellas flip with a floppy flair.

Warmth and joy in a playful blend,
Nature's giggle where wishes ascend.
A splash of whimsy, a dash of delight,
Soft sunshower magic, a whimsical sight.

Join the dance of the droplets' play,
In this gentle shower, come what may.
Every raindrop whispers a quirk,
In this elegance where laughter lurks.

Dappled Radiance

In the garden, quirky rays,
Dancing shadows, sunny plays.
A citrus twist on the sill,
Makes each moment a little thrill.

Bees in shades of yellow swirl,
Wings a-flutter, they twirl and whirl.
A pair of socks on a bright spout,
Oh dear, what's that all about?

Chasing blooms with chipper grace,
Giggles echo, a silly race.
Who knew that joy could take such flight,
In a patch that shines so bright?

Hats that wobble, laughter flows,
Tickled petals, a bloom that glows.
With every giggle, the worlds collide,
In dappled radiance, we take pride.

Curdled Sunshine

A glass of joy, with bits of cheer,
Sipping laughter, loud and clear.
Wobbling jello on a bright dish,
What a strange and wacky wish!

Scrambled moments on a plate,
Sunny yolk turns up the fate.
Flip that pancake, watch it fly,
Oh my, watch that batter shy!

Throwing bits of zest around,
In the mix, sheer fun is found.
Pancakes flipping, syrup glides,
Curdled scenes that laughter hides.

Muffins bouncing with a grin,
A burst of giggles from within.
What's for breakfast? Pure delight,
In the kitchen, nothing's slight.

Festooned with Zest

Sundaes topped with striped delight,
Sprinkles dancing in pure light.
Whipped cream swirls with a wink,
What a colorful way to think!

Napkins tucked, ties askew,
This party's brewing something new.
With every slice, a giggle spreads,
Laughter shared with silly threads.

Balloons floating, colors bright,
Squeezed-out juice, oh what a sight!
Fake mustaches and goofy hats,
Create a stir, with friendly chats.

A splash of zest, a wink or two,
Let's share a cake, just me and you.
Life's a laugh, let's make it grand,
In a festooned world, hand in hand.

Botanical Whirls

In a patch of quirky greens,
Tickled ferns and comical scenes.
Lopsy daisy, giggling low,
What a funny way to grow!

Whirly twirls in a leafy dance,
Petals blushing, miss a chance.
Bouncing sprouts with leafy flair,
Nature's jesters everywhere.

Wacky weeds that dance and play,
With muddy boots, we blend the day.
Grab a flower, wear it proud,
In botanical whirls, we're crowd!

Jubilant jumps through tangles grow,
Sharing secrets soft and slow.
With every chuckle, joys unfurl,
In our silly, plant-filled whirl.

Threads of Zing

In a world of vibrant hue,
I tossed a joke or two.
With fabric bright and bold,
Wrapped in laughter, tales unfold.

A stitch of quirk, a quirky seam,
Where giggles burst like a sunbeam.
Crafted chaos, oh so grand,
In this wacky wonderland.

Bobbin and thread, a dance of cheer,
Swirling whispers, drawing near.
With every twirl and playful twist,
Life's a circus, can't resist!

So let's embrace this wiggly thread,
With puns and pippins, we're well-fed.
In a tapestry of glee,
We sew our fun, just you and me!

Juicy Petal Confections

A treat of taste, so sweet and round,
In laughter's kitchen, joy is found.
Frosted giggles, sprinkles of fun,
Sipping bubble tea, oh what a run!

With a splash of zest, I bake a cake,
Giggles rise, make no mistake.
In the oven, smiles do swell,
With each bite, we cast a spell.

Candied dreams and silly shouts,
Giving way to hearty clouts.
Sugar-coated whimsy on a plate,
Let's celebrate, isn't it great?

So bring your forks and spoons afresh,
A banquet of joy's our tasty mesh.
With every plate, we'll laugh and cheer,
Juicy petals, we hold dear!

Sunlit Frills

In a garden where giggles bloom,
Frilly skirts chase away the gloom.
Dancing shadows in bright sunbeams,
Twisting joy like playful dreams.

With every twirl, a breeze ignites,
Giddy whispers, fluttering lights.
Navigate the grassy maze,
In sunlight's warmth, we love to graze.

Puffy clouds and polka-dots,
Giggles spark in sunny spots.
Come join this merry little dance,
As we prance beneath the chance.

With every step, there's fun to sniff,
Let laughter sail, like a lively riff.
In frills and thrills, we find our place,
With beaming hearts, let's leave a trace!

The Citrus Embrace

A zesty hug where chuckles blend,
A squeeze of fun; the day won't end.
With playful puns and tasty yums,
We spark the joy and dance like drums.

In sunshine's glow, with zest we play,
Mixing laughter in every way.
Juicy tales and giggly bites,
Brighten up our many nights.

So come enjoy this vibrant cheer,
With bubbly drinks and smiles sincere.
A citrus kiss upon the cheek,
Laughing out loud is what we seek!

With every sip, our spirits rise,
In this embrace, no room for sighs.
So lift your glass, let laughter flare,
In this zesty joy, we freely share!

Zesty Serenade in Echoing Patterns

A twist of citrus brings a grin,
With sassy loops that dare to spin.
The laughter's sharp, a playful tease,
As flavors dance upon the breeze.

A frothy swirl of bright delight,
In silly hats that fly in flight.
With giggles popping like the fizz,
Each note a burst of joyful whiz.

The antics of the tangy treat,
With every step, a shuffling beat.
In vibrant tones and bouncy steps,
Life's little joys are wide percepts.

So raise a glass, let's toast the cheer,
With citrus smiles that disappear.
We'll sing a song of jests and glee,
In every slice, sweet jubilee.

The Essence of Sunshine Wrapped in Elegance

Golden rays in fabric bright,
Twirl and shimmer, pure delight.
With fancy frills that catch the eye,
A joyful swirl that makes us sigh.

The humor drips like melted cream,
A fancy dance, a waking dream.
With every stitch, a chuckle grows,
In patterns wild, the laughter flows.

Wrapped in charm, it's quite a sight,
With twirls and flips that feel just right.
A sunny jig in evening light,
Life's grand delight, oh what a night!

So let's embrace this vibrant hue,
Where elegance meets silly too.
With playful steps and hearty cheer,
We'll make this moment last all year.

Sugar and Spice in Fragile Threads

A dash of whimsy, sweet and bold,
In threads so fine, stories unfold.
With giggles stitched both here and there,
A fabric world beyond compare.

Spicy banter in every seam,
A frolic fit for any dream.
With funny patches, quirky styles,
Each twist and turn brings radiant smiles.

The textures play, a vibrant mix,
A goofy jive, a gleeful fix.
In patterns bright and colors wild,
A zany dance, the heart of a child.

So wrap me up in this delight,
Where sugar's sweet and spice feels right.
In every thread, a laugh we find,
A tapestry of joyful mind.

Captured Sunshine in Ethereal Fabric

In gauzy threads, the sun does weave,
A playful waltz that won't deceive.
With each flutter, a giggle waits,
As sunlight dances on the gates.

A shimmer here, a sparkle there,
In whimsical duds that float in air.
With twinkling eyes and playful grace,
We chase the joy in every space.

Captured moments, bright and light,
Unruly fun that feels just right.
With every twist, a twirling spree,
Life's crazy joys, eternally free.

So come and join this jolly romp,
In fabric dreams where we all stomp.
With laughter spun from golden rays,
We'll treasure this in endless ways.

Radiant Filigree

In a world where zest takes flight,
Frilly frocks spin day and night.
Slicing giggles with a grin,
Twirling madly, let's begin!

Bubbling laughter fills the air,
As colors clash without a care.
Lemon squishes, frothy cheer,
What a sight, it's crystal clear!

Dresses twirl like tarts on plates,
Whimsical patterns—what a fate!
Witty words and zesty puns,
Woven tales that crack like guns!

Every twinkle in the sun,
Whirls of fun have just begun.
In this maze of laughter's play,
Join the dance, don't shy away!

Citrus Blossom Veil

Bubbly like a soda pop,
Joyful prancing, can't quite stop.
With a swirl and cheerful skip,
Jokes on arms like candy strip!

Hats adorned with sassy flair,
Bright as moonlight on a dare.
Sipping giggles, tasting zest,
Who knew antics could be best?

Frothy whispers, playful tease,
Dancing clumsily with ease.
While the sun shines on our gig,
We'll play tag with orange swig!

Chasing shadows, running free,
In this world of jubilee.
Wrapped in laughter's tender glow,
Spinning tales as wild winds blow!

Sweet Citrus Mosaic

Patchwork quilts of tasty fun,
Sunshine splashes—everyone!
Color clashes in delight,
Tickling fancies, feeling bright!

Juggling fruit with joyful cheer,
Flavored giggles, can you hear?
Mixing flavors, loud parade,
Tickled toes in sunshine made!

Chasing cheeky butterflies,
With zestful laughs and happy sighs.
Building castles made of dreams,
On a sea of sunny beams!

Swirls of fun like ribbons chase,
Every smile's a warm embrace.
In this world of sweet surprise,
Laughter dances, never lies!

Tender Twists

Twists and twirls in liquid gold,
Stories shared and laughter bold.
With a wink and joyful dance,
What's a party without a chance?

Sipping sunshine, all aglow,
Fruity flavors steal the show.
Matching shoes all out of whack,
Spinning tales that burst and crack!

Lively chatter fills the room,
Bouncing feet dispel all gloom.
Citrusy curls bounce and sway,
Leave your worries, come and play!

Every chuckle leaves a trace,
In this wacky, bright embrace.
Come and twirl into the night,
With tender twists, it feels just right!

Gossamer Citrus Dreams

In a garden, bright and playful,
A creature danced, quite whimsical.
With a grin like sunshine,
And a twist of zest divine.

The bees wore hats, all striped and proud,
While butterflies giggled, flying loud.
They sipped from dew like fine champagne,
Tickling petals in the rain.

A jester jumped, wearing citrus shoes,
Spinning tales with silly views.
His sidekick, a twirling grape,
Chasing giggles in a caped escape.

Finding joy in every bite,
As laughter sprinkles day and night.
In wild dreams, we frolic free,
In this quirky jubilee.

Tapestry of Tang

A patch of yellow, bright allure,
Woven threads of joy so pure.
A tickle here, a wink there,
Spinning tales in the summer air.

Silly socks on rolling hills,
Dancing under spinning wheels.
The sun was lemon, the laughter sweet,
As starlings chirped a rhythmic beat.

Frisky wind with a giggle kissed,
As breezes chased a twinkling mist.
On grass we tumbled, quick and spry,
With clouds above, we'd leap and fly.

A tapestry of joy spun 'round,
Each thread a tale of laughter found.
In vibrant hues of pure delight,
We danced beneath the pale moonlight.

Silken Brightness

In a bowl, a mix of cheer,
Glistening fruits, so bright, so near.
Silken trails of sweetness glide,
While giggles burst from deep inside.

A split banana, wearing hats,
Laughing with a bunch of chats.
Frothy drinks with fluffy straws,
Riding waves of tasty laws.

A sprinkle here, a wink of zest,
Silly games, we laugh the best.
In a sunny patch we play,
Whispers of joy, like a cabernet.

Embroidery of flavors swirls,
As laughter dances, giggles twirls.
With every bite, new joys unfold,
In silken shades of bright and bold.

Golden Delicacies

A shimmering feast with hues of gold,
Tales of laughter in bites untold.
Pies that giggle, tarts that glow,
Each a rhythm, a happy show.

Peels that twirled like ballerinas,
With every crunch, a burst of glee is.
Dipped in honey, oh so sweet,
Jovial dances with every treat.

In kitchens bright, a band would play,
As wafts of citrus danced away.
With every smile, the table's set,
For moments we'd never forget.

Golden treasures in every dish,
Drizzled joy is our only wish.
With forks that prance and spoons that sing,
A feast of laughter is the real king.

Gleaming Citrus Fragrance

A burst of zest in the noon sun,
With every twist, the giggles run.
Sipping joy from a quirky mug,
Those pouts and grins, oh what a tug!

Mirth spills forth from wrinkled skin,
In this world, we dance and spin.
Our taste buds tickle, wild and free,
A citrus cheer, just you and me.

Tickling tongues with a splash of cheer,
We pop and fizz, can you hear?
Frothy bubbles in crazy whirl,
We're the quirkiest mix in the swirl!

With every sip, the world feels bright,
A juicy laugh in sheer delight.
Wrapped in sunshine, what a craze,
In this gleaming, zesty haze.

Touch of Gold

A golden slice in a happy place,
Smiles and laughter, a cheerful race.
Dancing peels on a kitchen floor,
A fruity treasure, who could ask for more?

Twist and shout with flamboyant flair,
A buttery touch that fills the air.
With every chuckle, we toast a cheer,
For things that sparkle are always near.

Jokes are squeezed from every fruit,
Funny faces, who'd dare to dispute?
Rolling giggles, sweet and bold,
A legacy grand, more precious than gold!

In this delightful, fruity land,
With vibrant scenes so brightly planned.
Unruly zest, a lighthearted role,
A touch of joy to warm the soul.

Silken Embrace

In a wardrobe bright, we find our glee,
A fabric twist, oh so merry!
Silken whispers wrapped around us,
Witty banter, a fun-filled fuss.

Threads of laughter we weave so tight,
Crafting moments that feel just right.
With swirls and curls, we prance about,
In a joyful dance, there's no doubt!

Tantalizing fabrics, bright like sun,
Every thread tells a tale of fun.
In sheer delight, we play the game,
Draped in joy, never the same!

A silken embrace of friendship's cheer,
Woven tight, we banish fear.
Fashioned from laughter, woven tight,
Together, we shine, pure delight.

Sweet Fragrance Trails

A scent that trails, oh what a tease,
Winding pathways through the trees.
Curly giggles on a breezy day,
Spinning stories, come what may!

Whispers of joy in the morning light,
Ticklish breezes, a pure delight.
With teasing smells that dance around,
Every corner, happiness found!

Silly winks in the fragrant air,
Chasing clouds without a care.
Following trails of zest and cheer,
Funny moments, drawing near!

In this world of scents and grace,
We sprinkle joy in every place.
A sweet perfume, a laughing game,
In playful antics, we stake our claim.

Tangy Elegance

In a garden bright with zesty cheer,
A playful breeze does twirl and steer,
A hat adorned with citrus zest,
Who knew elegance could jest?

With twinkling eyes and giggles near,
A lady prances, rotary gear,
Her shoes slip on a sticky floor,
And now she's dancing, oh what a score!

The sun peeks through with a golden hue,
As friends gather 'round, a motley crew,
Each one armed with a sun-kissed grin,
Who knew mischief could wear such skin?

A toast to folly, a toast to fun,
In this wild world, we've all but won,
For who would dare to wear a frown,
When tangy treats are spinning 'round?

Hued Petals

A splash of color, oh what a sight,
Petals bold, glimmering bright,
A clumsy bee hits the party hard,
Turns out he's just a bit off guard!

In this frolic of colors wide,
A prankster tickles the butterfly's side,
With winks and jests, the petals sway,
Who knew flowers could play all day?

The sunbeam giggles, bouncing light,
As bees do jive and tease a flight,
Laughter erupts from every bloom,
Whispers of joy erupt in the room!

It's a carnival of nature's grace,
Where silly dances set the pace,
Forget convention, take a chance,
In this wild world, we'll laugh and prance!

Sweet and Sour Dance

With a twist of fate and a zany waltz,
A jester spins, and nothing faults,
Sweetness drips from every hand,
While sour notes craft a band!

Around the table, laughter blooms,
As friends recall those silly dooms,
A pie too tart, a lemonade splash,
Each sip becomes a zesty clash.

The dance begins, with raised eyebrows,
All partake, no time to rouse,
Who knew a twist could cause such grins?
In this parade, we're all good friends!

So raise a cup, let laughter flow,
With sweet and sour, high and low,
In this dance of fun, we'll prance about,
With joy loudly muffled, and hearts full of clout!

Yellow Charms

With sunbeam smiles and splashes bold,
A charming tale is being told,
A friend, a quip, a zesty laugh,
Together we'll write our own epitaph!

A yellow hat with a feather bright,
Rides along with pure delight,
As giggles bubble, round and round,
Who knew charm could be so profound?

A poke here, a twist there,
This lighthearted game gives quite a scare,
With slips and trips, oh what a sight,
In a swirl of humor, we find the light!

With candy hearts and jokes to share,
In this garden party, we declare,
For every chuckle, a bond to adore,
In our yellow joys, we'll laugh some more!

The Bright Mosaic

A twist of yellow in the bowl,
A sight that tickles, lights the soul.
Funny faces all around,
With every bite, laughter is found.

Pies and cakes in a wild array,
Dancing flavors come out to play.
Spoonfuls of joy and a squirt of zest,
Who knew fruit could be such a jest?

Hats made of rinds on silly heads,
Bouncing giggles in sunny spreads.
Sticky fingers, brightened grins,
Juggling treasures, let the fun begin!

Colorful bites, a sweet parade,
In this zestful ambiance, we wade.
Bubbling laughter, fruity delight,
Mosaic of joy in the fading light.

Whimsical Sunlight Dance

A splash of fun in a radiant jar,
Twirling sunlight, what a bizarre!
Chasing shadows, giggles in bloom,
Bouncing around in the living room.

With spritz of joy, the air so bright,
Doodles of flavor in every bite.
Silly hats that bounce and swing,
Who knew fruit could make you sing?

Dancing spoons, an orchestra of cheer,
Melodies made of laughter and beer.
Jumping jigs to a fruity beat,
Life is juicy, oh, what a treat!

In the kitchen, smiles so wide,
Splashes of color, all bona fide.
Whimsical tales unfold in the sun,
With every grin, we have so much fun!

Emblazoned with Citrus

Bright little balls of sunshine cheer,
Calling out, 'Come, gather near!'
Tangy bites and bubbly sips,
Wiggly giggles from happy lips.

Jokes are sprinkled with zestful glee,
As we create our culinary spree.
Punning around with every slice,
Oh, these fruits are more than nice!

A hat made of peels, a dance with flair,
Each one tries on their fruity wear.
Jelly beans in a citrus town,
Watch out world, we're turning it brown!

Every squeeze brings a new good cheer,
Emblazoned with joy, don't you dare fear.
Flavorful frolics in each bright hue,
Mixing and mashing, a zesty crew!

Dappled Delight

Sprinkles of yellow, a feathery touch,
A giggly charm that means so much.
Citrusy pow-wows, a round of applause,
Each laugh harder than a joke with no cause.

Sticky hands and wobbly knees,
Crafting treats with fruity ease.
Bouncing flavors in a jolly mix,
A zany dance, nature's funny tricks.

In the garden, the fruits all play,
Winking shadows in bright disarray.
Giggles explode, a zesty spree,
As we concoct our own harmony.

With every morsel, joy ignites,
A merry dance in summer nights.
Dappled delight in flavors divine,
Come join the frolic, it's party time!

Radiant Hues in Ethereal Patterns

In the garden where colors clash,
Bright yellow blooms do a cheeky flash.
A swish of fabric, with laughter's tune,
Twisting and twirling, in afternoon.

Underneath a sky of playful cheer,
A twist of whimsy, the moment near.
Bright shades colliding in silly delight,
With every twirl, they take flight.

A splash of brightness, oh what a sight,
Stitching together the day and night.
Clashing patterns dance in a grin,
Laughter is sewn in, let the fun begin.

In this kaleidoscope of bright surprise,
Fabric of joy, where humor lies.
Ride the rhythm, a whimsical chase,
For in this world, we're woven with grace.

Touched by Sunshine

On the windowsill sits a cheeky smile,
Golden rays stretch, basking for a while.
Tickled by warmth with a wink and a tease,
Giggles galore, as they flutter like leaves.

A dance of shadows that jiggle and sway,
Joy wraps around in a warm ballet.
With sparkles of sunlight, it's pure delight,
Each beam of laughter ignites the night.

Caught in the glow of a honeyed beam,
Shining like sequins in a whimsical dream.
Whispers of joy in rich yellow hues,
Cover the day like a playful muse.

Bright cherubs above with glee set afloat,
As the breeze sings sweetly, a happy note.
In every sunbeam, there's a story spun,
A tapestry woven, always having fun.

Bound by Grace

Tangled threads with a giggly twist,
Sassy and silly, they can't resist.
A flick of fabric, a chuckle in sight,
Dancing together, all day and night.

Stitches of humor in patterns so bold,
Whispers of laughter, both daring and cold.
Bound in a hug of a bright cotton swirl,
Creating a puzzle, a playful whirl.

In a world where the quirky abide,
Woven together, they simply can't hide.
Each seam a story, woven with care,
A whimsical quilt, oh what a flare!

As mismatched pieces come together and glow,
A spectacle brimming with jovial flow.
With joy in each stitch, they gallivant place,
In the fabric of moments, we find our grace.

Threads of Joy in Zesty Clarity

A splash of zing, an effervescent flair,
Waves of bright shades swirling in air.
Each thread bursting forth like a beam,
Crafting a canvas where giggles teem.

Patches of cheer on a bold parade,
Laughter wraps round like a sweet cascade.
In every fold, a twist of delight,
Zesty creations that shine ever bright.

Joyful yarns in a dance of sass,
A quirky fabric that calls out 'class!'
Colors collide in a merry embrace,
Sending ripples of glee, a playful trace.

Patterns of whimsy, sewing the air,
Spreading joy like sunshine everywhere.
Each thread a chuckle, each stitch a song,
In the realm of fabrics, we all belong.

The Scent of Citrus Amidst Soft Textiles

Soft shadows mingle with a zesty glow,
Fabrics dance lightly, putting on a show.
In a whirl of colors, laughter ignites,
While lemons and laces tease our sights.

A splash of freshness, a wink overhead,
With giggles wrapped up in every thread.
Sunshine and fabric, a comedy act,
A laugh riot sewn, that's a matter of fact.

Citrusy scents in the playful air,
Tickling the senses, beyond compare.
In this universe of soft delight,
Joy threads together, day and night.

So don't be shy, join the quirky spree,
Let every stitch sing, and just be free.
In this world so bright, we'll find our way,
Wrapped in the warmth of a funny play.

Whispers of Brightness

In a garden full of cheer,
A fruit has much to say,
With a grin so wide and bright,
It dances on its way.

Friends gather near in glee,
With sips of bubbly cheer,
A twist makes all things jolly,
We laugh away our fear.

A pie on the table sings,
With scents that tickle noses,
A slice of joy, it brings,
As everyone composes.

So raise a cup to sunny days,
To goofy, silly fun,
For when life gives a zestful twist,
We find we all have won.

Draped in Sunlight

Fabrics bright and bold,
In patterns that amuse,
An outfit woven sunny,
With laughter as the muse.

The stitches jiggle, dance,
Each thread a playful tease,
Whispers of the sunlit bounce,
With every funky breeze.

Underneath the sun's bright rays,
We twirl in smiles and beams,
A fashion show of witticisms,
As silly as our dreams.

So twirl and sway, my friends,
In colors loud and bright,
For every stitch a giggle's worth,
In the golden light.

Ambrosial Patterns

On a table set with flair,
Delights in bright array,
A dance of tastes unfolds,
To brighten up our play.

Dishes swirl with fun and zest,
Flavors jiggle and laugh,
A fiesta in the kitchen,
As we devour the aftermath.

Forks and spoons are in a race,
Who can grab the best?
With every bite, we chuckle loud,
In a hearty, joyful fest.

So serve the sprightly flavors bold,
In laughter's sweet embrace,
For dining is a merry tale,
That keeps the grin on pace.

Twirls of Zesty Delight

A twist upon the dance floor,
With humor as our guide,
We spin and laugh together,
In a zesty, gleeful glide.

With citrus in our pockets,
And a wink upon our face,
We whirl in silly movements,
Find laughter in the chase.

Each turn's a splash of color,
A burst of joy and cheer,
With every leap and giggle,
We shake away our fear.

So come and join the twirl,
With mischief in our sight,
For the world blooms humorously,
In these zesty beams of light.

Zesty Ribbons

In a garden of giggles, I twirl and spin,
With ribbons of citrus, let the games begin.
A wink from a daisy, a chuckle from thyme,
We dance with the quirky, in rhythm and rhyme.

Oh, fruity concoctions in hats so absurd,
A parrot in spectacles, it's truly unheard!
With each silly prance, we elude all despair,
Painting the day with a citrusy flair.

Like confetti that tumbles, we scatter around,
Chasing the laughter, with nary a frown.
In capers and capers, the merriment grows,
While zesty concoctions spill bright through our toes.

So take off your shoes, let the giggles take flight,
With each step we take, let's ignite the delight!
These ribbons of zazz, they won't come undone,
In this wacky parade, we'll laugh 'til we're done.

Bursting Petals

Out in the meadow, where oddities bloom,
Petals burst forth with a tickling zoom.
They've donned funny hats, and they wiggle with glee,
A conga of daisies, just wait 'til you see!

Confused by the sunshine, the tulips stand tall,
Sporting big smiles like they're ready to ball.
A giggle escapes from the pansies so bright,
As they twirl in the breeze, what a whimsical sight!

Sprinkling joy, the petals ignite,
With skits by the sun, we dance day and night.
In this floral ballet, no frown should remain,
As cossets of bobbles rain down like confetti rain.

Let's pop like balloons, in this zany affair,
With giggles and dances that float in the air.
For humor's a garden, where laughter can bloom,
In a world full of petals, we'll shatter the gloom!

Sunkissed Embroidery

Threads of laughter weave through the air,
With patterns of mischief that dance without care.
Sunkissed and quirky, the garments all sway,
As I stitch up the giggles in a bright, silly way.

I've sewn on a pocket, a pouch full of grins,
With pockets of sunshine and sparkles within.
Knots of whimsy tie tales that delight,
As we frolic in fabric, from morning 'til night.

Each hem tells a story, of joy and of cheer,
While buttons, like marbles, roll free without fear.
In this quilt of the unusual, how vibrant the hues,
With stitches of laughter, our hearts wear the news!

So come join this party where tulle meets the twist,
With strands of humor, we dare to insist.
In colors so zany that colors can't find,
We'll wrap up in joy, let old worries unwind.

Ethereal Zest

In a world of odd flavors, where giggles are sweet,
There's laughter-infused joy, a quirky little treat.
With sprinkles of chuckles and whimsy galore,
We sprinkle on frolic, forever wanting more.

The air holds a story, a breeze full of laughs,
With zest that's contagious, like playful giraffes.
They leap through the pages of stories untold,
In this feast of the funny, we eat up the bold!

Twisting and turning, our spirits unite,
With flavors of fun, we soar like a kite.
In swirls of the unusual, we savor the jest,
With giggles and zest, we are truly the best.

So hold on to joy, let it bubble and brew,
With an essence of laughter, where skies are so blue.
In this whimsical realm, where laughter takes flight,
We'll dance in the zest, 'til the end of the night.

The Golden Symphony

In a land where laughter beams,
Yellow hats and sunny dreams,
Dancers twirl in zestful glee,
Playing songs of joy to see.

Pies that bounce with citrus zest,
Squeeze the juice, it's all the best!
Bouncy balls on polished floors,
Who knew fun could open doors?

Tickled tongues and giggles bright,
While the sun prepares for night,
A symphony of tasty tunes,
Whistling through the afternoon!

As the laughter takes its flight,
We're all wrapped in vibes so right,
With a pinch of silly spark,
We laugh until it's nearly dark.

Timeless Yellows

A twist of humor in the air,
Golden curls and an orange chair,
Slipping on a mustard floor,
What else could we ask for?

Juggling joy, a comical jest,
Chasing shadows, feeling blessed,
Wraps of sunshine spinning round,
In this happy, silly sound.

With every smile, a wink, a wave,
These sunny moments we all crave,
Sipping punch with paper straws,
Can you hear our raucous applause?

Timeless giggles fill the scene,
In shades of yellow, pure and keen,
Who knew the hue could entertain?
Bubbly laughs inside the rain?

Mosaic of Sunlit Flavors

A patchwork quilt of laughter thrives,
Where each slice of sunshine jives,
Sassy smiles on every face,
Craft a magic, swirly place.

With fruity treats and playful cheer,
We throw our doubts into the sphere,
A swirl of giggles, oh so fine,
Taste the joy from every vine!

Puddles of color, crazy and bright,
We dance and sing beneath the light,
Mixing flavors like a dream,
Soda pops that burst and beam.

In a world of zesty clashes,
Every moment, humor splashes,
Loving life with joyful hearts,
In this mosaic, joy imparts!

Elusive Citrus Patterns

Whimsical sprites in lemonade,
With tickles and silliness laid,
Patterns dance in sunlight's grace,
Every corner has a face!

A squirt of bliss, a pop of cheer,
In the air, giggles appear,
While fruity tales spin around,
Silly stories abound!

Jumping jests like frothy waves,
Through a maze that our heart craves,
Sticky fingers, lemon smears,
Welcome laughter through the years!

In this dizzy, twisty space,
Oh, how we embrace the race!
Chasing laughter, chasing light,
Elusive patterns take a flight.

Delicate Citrus Whisper

A fruit so bright, it smiles with glee,
In the sunlight, it dances free.
It teases taste buds, sharp yet sweet,
With every bite, it's quite the treat.

A tiny twist, a merry jest,
It rolls around, just like a pest.
With every squirt, it's full of fun,
A citrus prank that's never done.

A Twist of Zest

A riddle wrapped, a peel so sly,
It'll make you laugh, oh my, oh my!
With every twist, a giggle grows,
The tangy burst, the humor flows.

It frolics in a glass of cheer,
Mixing drinks, it volunteers.
A curious blend that can't be beat,
A zesty laugh, a splendid treat.

Fragile Sunshine

A shimmer bright as morning dew,
In fragile hues, a radiant view.
With every squinch, it lights the room,
A glow of joy, no hint of gloom.

It sits on cakes, a fancied sight,
Its playful tartness brings delight.
A slice of giggles, light and spry,
It whispers joy, oh my, oh my!

Fabrics of Flavor

A tapestry of zest unfurls,
With swirls of tang among the pearls.
In every stitch, a little grin,
A dance of taste, let's dive right in.

It drapes the plate in sunny cheer,
A lace of flavors drawing near.
With every bite, a playful jest,
A quirky feast, we're truly blessed.

www.ingramcontent.com/pod-product-compliance
Lightning Source LLC
Chambersburg PA
CBHW051735290426
43661CB00123B/341